MW01115366

Desert Life

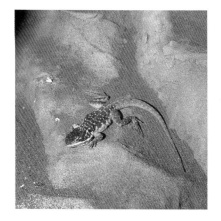

Focus: Habitats

Meredith Costain

Deserts are dry and hot.
But desert plants and
animals store water
and stay cool.

This is a stone plant.
It stores water in its leaves.

This is a cactus.
It stores water in its stem.

This is a camel.
It stores water in its hump.

This is a desert mouse.
It makes water
from its food.

These are desert foxes.
They come out at night
to stay cool.

This is a desert lizard.
It has scaly skin
to stay cool.